MW00954858

A GIFT TO YOU FROM THE

## Saint Peter
### Public Library
Saint Peter

# It's a Tornado!

## by Nadia Higgins

## illustrated by Damian Ward

Content Consultant: Steven A. Ackerman
Professor of Atmospheric Science
University of Wisconsin–Madison

# visit us at www.abdopublishing.com

Published by Magic Wagon, a division of the ABDO Group, 8000 West 78th Street, Edina, Minnesota 55439. Copyright © 2010 by Abdo Consulting Group, Inc. International copyrights reserved in all countries. All rights reserved. No part of this book may be reproduced in any form without written permission from the publisher.

Looking Glass Library™ is a trademark and logo of Magic Wagon.

Printed in the United States of America, North Mankato, Minnesota.
092009
012010

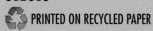 PRINTED ON RECYCLED PAPER

Text by Nadia Higgins
Illustrations by Damian Ward
Edited by Mari Kesselring
Interior layout and design by Nicole Brecke
Cover design by Becky Daum

**Library of Congress Cataloging-in-Publication Data**
Higgins, Nadia.
  It's a tornado! / by Nadia Higgins ; illustrated by Damian Ward ; content consultant, Steven A. Ackerman.
       p. cm. — (Weather watchers)
  Includes index.
  ISBN 978-1-60270-730-6
  1. Tornadoes—Juvenile literature.  I. Ward, Damian, 1977- ill. II. Title.
  QC955.2.H54 2010
  551.55'3—dc22
                                        2009029375

# Table of Contents

# It's a Tornado!

It is creepy outside. The air is hot and sticky. The sky is dark. You can hear thunder rumbling.

A tornado is coming!

A tornado is a very fast wind. It spins and spins. You can see a tornado. It is long and skinny. It hangs from a dark cloud.

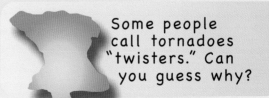

Some people call tornadoes "twisters." Can you guess why?

# A Giant Vacuum Cleaner

A tornado works like a giant vacuum cleaner. It sucks up dirt and branches. A very strong tornado can suck up cars. It can blow apart buildings. Then, the pieces fall back down.

A tornado can take the feathers off a chicken. It can also suck milk out of an open jug.

During a tornado, windows break. Branches, garbage cans, and other things fly through the air.

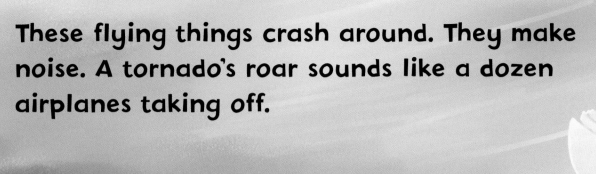

These flying things crash around. They make noise. A tornado's roar sounds like a dozen airplanes taking off.

A tornado can tear the wall off a house. But, the furniture inside could be okay!

A tornado travels over
land. It makes a path.
Things just outside
the path may not
be touched.

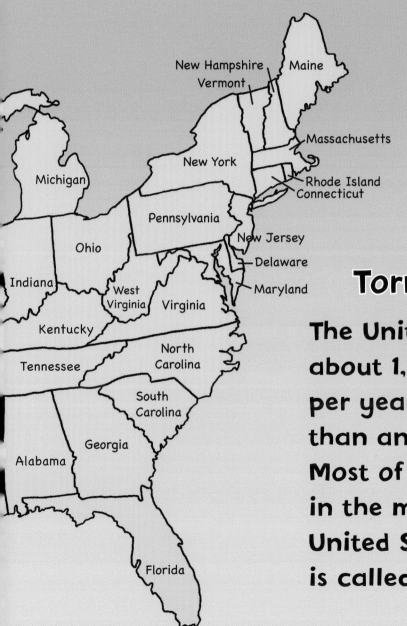

# Tornado Alley

The United States has about 1,500 tornadoes per year. That is more than any other country. Most of these happen in the middle of the United States. This area is called Tornado Alley.

In Tornado Alley, tornadoes mostly strike in April, May, and June. Tornadoes can occur anytime during the day. But they happen most often in the early evening.

# A Storm Is Born

Tornadoes come from thunderclouds.

Warm, wet air blows in near the ground. Cold air moves in above. These air masses meet. The warm air shoots up quickly. A huge thundercloud forms.

Air inside the thundercloud begins to spin. The spinning air drops down. It is a funnel cloud. If the funnel touches the ground, it is a tornado.

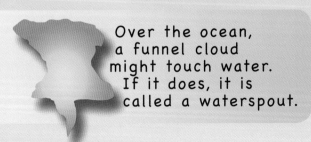

Over the ocean, a funnel cloud might touch water. If it does, it is called a waterspout.

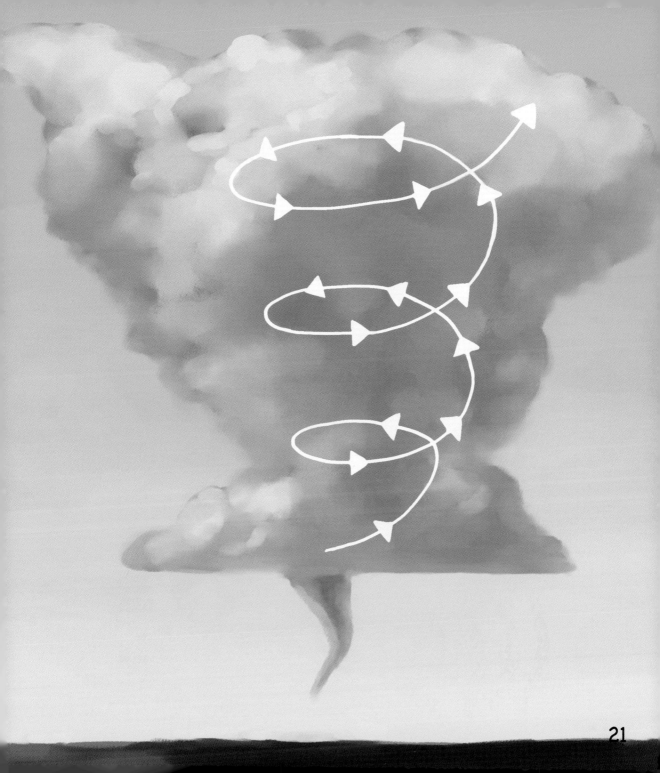

DOPPLER RADAR

Storm chasers drive around looking for tornadoes. They study the tornadoes close-up.

# Spotting Storms

Only a few thunderclouds cause tornadoes. Which ones are they? Scientists can tell.

One tool they use is Doppler radar. It measures the wind's speed and direction.

# Tornado Watch

Scientists can often tell when a tornado is coming. They issue a tornado watch. People can learn about the storm from the news on the radio and television.

Tornadoes can happen in many places. Check with an adult to see if tornadoes have hit your area. Make a plan for what to do during a tornado.

# Tornado Warning!

When a tornado has been spotted, the watch becomes a tornado warning. Blaring sirens warn people!

The safest place during a tornado is a basement. The next best places are inside a closet or bathroom on the first story. Always stay away from windows during a tornado.

# Safe!

After the warning is over, it is safe to leave your shelter. If you weren't in the tornado's path, you missed some of the strongest winds on Earth!

# How a Tornado Forms

1. During a storm, winds near the ground blow in one direction. Winds higher above the ground blow in the other direction.

2. The opposite winds create a rotating air mass, or a funnel.

3. The funnel drops down from the clouds. It touches the ground and becomes a tornado.

# Tornado Facts

### A Record-Breaker
The deadliest single tornado in U.S. history happened on March 18, 1925. The storm swept over Missouri, Illinois, and Indiana. Nobody knew it was coming. Almost 700 people died.

### Measuring Tornadoes
The strength of a tornado is measured using the Enhanced Fujita Scale. It rates the wind speed of a tornado on a scale from 0 to 5. A very strong tornado will have a 5.

### All 50
Every state in the United States has had at least one tornado. At 139 per year, Texas gets the most. Alaska and Rhode Island get the fewest.

# Glossary

**air mass** — a body of air with a certain temperature and humidity.
**Doppler radar** — a tool that scientists use to find tornadoes and track storms.
**funnel cloud** — a spinning cloud that hangs down from another, larger cloud. It is smaller on the bottom than on the top.
**thundercloud** — a huge, dark cloud that can cause hail, thunderstorms, and tornadoes.

# On the Web

To learn more about tornadoes, visit ABDO Group online at **www.abdopublishing.com**. Web sites about tornadoes are featured on our Book Links page. These links are routinely monitored and updated to provide the most current information available.

# Index